Discover India
State by State

OFF TO KERALA

SONIA MEHTA

PUFFIN BOOKS

An imprint of Penguin Random House

PUFFIN BOOKS

USA | Canada | UK | Ireland | Australia | New Zealand | India | South Africa | China | Singapore

Puffin Books is part of the Penguin Random House group of companies whose addresses can be found at global.penguinrandomhouse.com

Published by Penguin Random House India Pvt. Ltd
4th Floor, Capital Tower 1, MG Road,
Gurugram 122 002, Haryana, India

Penguin
Random House
India

First published in Puffin Books by Penguin Random House India 2017

Text, design and illustrations copyright © Quadrum Solutions Pvt. Ltd 2017
Series copyright © Penguin Random House India 2017

Picture Credits
P 14: Thiruvananthapuram, Kerala (Manu M Nair/Shutterstock.com); P 15: Kozhikode (© Dhruvaraj S from India (Calicut Beach) [CC BY 2.0 (http://creativecommons.org/licenses/by/2.0)], via Wikimedia Commons); P 16: Ruins of the building of Panamaram Jain Temple, Wayanad, Kerala (ManeeshUpadhyay/Shutterstock.com), Carvings of Ashoka (By Photo Dharma from Sadao, Thailand [CC BY 2.0 (http://creativecommons.org/licenses/by/2.0)], via Wikimedia Commons); P 20-21: Kerala backwaters (CRS PHOTO/Shutterstock.com); P 22: Man painting his face (silentwings/Shutterstock.com), Writings on Palm leaves (AjayTvm/Shutterstock.com); p 24: Mohiniattam dancer (Zzvet/Shutterstock.com), Kathakali dancer (Dmytro Gilitukha/Shutterstock.com); P 25: Ottamthullal dancer (© Sai K shanmugam (Own work) [CC BY-SA 3.0 (http://creativecommons.org/licenses/by-sa/3.0)], via Wikimedia Commons); P 27: Boat race (Rajesh Narayanan/Shutterstock.com), Pooran celebrations (AJP/Shutterstock.com); P 28: British Residency in Kollam (© Arunvrparavur (Taken by me) [GFDL (http://www.gnu.org/copyleft/fdl.html) or CC BY-SA 4.0 (http://creativecommons.org/licenses/by-sa/4.0)], via Wikimedia Commons); P 29: A floor in traditional home (© Mithunphotography (Own work) [CC BY-SA 4.0 (http://creativecommons.org/licenses/by-sa/4.0)], via Wikimedia Commons); P 30: A veranda in a traditional home (© Sankarkeloth (Own work) [CC BY-SA 4.0 (http://creativecommons.org/licenses/by-sa/4.0)], via Wikimedia Commons), Pond (© Vinayaraj (Own work) [CC BY-SA 3.0 (http://creativecommons.org/licenses/by-sa/3.0)], via Wikimedia Commons), Granary (© Soumyavn [CC BY-SA 3.0 (http://creativecommons.org/licenses/by-sa/3.0)], via Wikimedia Commons), Courtyard (© Soumyavn [CC BY-SA 3.0 (http://creativecommons.org/licenses/by-sa/3.0)); P 34: Jewish Synagogue (© Deepujoseph [CC-BY-2.5 (https://creativecommons.org/licenses/by/2.5/deed.en)], via Wikimedia Commons), Thirunelli Temple (© Vijayakumarblathur (Own work) [CC BY-SA 3.0 (http://creativecommons.org/licenses/by-sa/3.0)], via Wikimedia Commons); P 37: Krishnapuram Palace (Manu M Nair/Shutterstock.com); P 40: A farmer from Kerala (© Challiyil Eswaramangalath Vipin from Chalakudy, India (a farmer from Kerala) [CC BY-SA 2.0 (http://creativecommons.org/licenses/by-sa/2.0)], via Wikimedia Commons); P 41: A fishing boat on the Malabar Coast (Daniel J. Rao/Shutterstock.com); P 42: Aranmula Kannadi (© Rajesh Nair from Bangalore, India (Aaranmula Kannadi) [CC BY 2.0 (http://creativecommons.org/licenses/by/2.0)], via Wikimedia Commons); P 45: Kootu Curry (© By Nairdeepa (Own work) [CC BY-SA 4.0 (http://creativecommons.org/licenses/by-sa/4.0)], via Wikimedia Commons); P 46: Puttu maker (© Augustus Binu [CC BY-SA 4.0 (http://creativecommons.org/licenses/by-sa/4.0)], via Wikimedia Commons)

The views and opinions expressed in this book are the author's own and the facts are as reported by her, which have been verified to the extent possible, and the publishers are not in any way liable for the same.

The information in this book is based on research from bona fide sites and published books and is true to the best of the author's knowledge at the time of going to print. The author is not responsible for any further changes or developments occurring post the publication of this book. This series is not a comprehensive representation of the states of India but is intended to give children a flavour of the lifestyles and cultures of different states. All illustrations are artistic representations only.

ISBN 9780143440925

Design and layout by Quadrum Solutions Pvt. Ltd
Printed at Repro India Limited

www.penguin.co.in

This is a legitimate digitally printed version of the book and therefore might not have certain extra finishing on the cover.

Hello Kids!

I'm so happy you are reading this book. India is an incredible country and there are lots of things about it that we never get to hear about.

I discovered India because my father was in the Indian army. He was posted to many places all over India—and we dutifully followed him. Can you imagine that by the time I was in the tenth standard, I had changed nine schools? Of course it was hard making new friends almost every year, but the good part was that I got to live in so many places. Right from Kerala, where I was born, to Kashmir, Jhansi, Shillong, Chandigarh, Goa . . . the list is long.

Every time I go to a new place, I feel amazed at how different each state is from the other—and yet, how similar. Did you know that we can see monuments from the Stone Age right here in India? Or that we have more than twenty official languages, and most Indians know three or four on an average? Or even that some of the world's most amazing scientific marvels were invented in India?

Oh, there are many, many, many fun and fantastic things about the states of India, which we simply must get to know.

So get your backpack ready, get set to meet some new friends, and join me on a fun trip as we DISCOVER INDIA, STATE BY STATE.

I hope you enjoy reading this book as much as I have enjoyed writing it. I would love to hear from you. So do write to me at sonia.mehta@quadrumltd.com.

Lots of love,
Sonia Aunty

Mishki and Pushka have come to visit Earth from their home planet, Zoomba. They have never seen such an amazing place. Zoomba doesn't have trees and mountains and rivers like Earth does. But the people look exactly the same. When they come to Earth, they meet a sweet old man whom they call Daadu Dolma. Daadu Dolma shows them all the wonderful places in India and tells Mishki and Pushka all about them.

Mishki and Pushka can't believe what they see. They have seen a lot of Earth, but they have never, ever seen a place like India.

They are off to explore India state by state :)

Mishki

Mishki is a curious little girl. She is always asking loads of questions. On her home planet, she is always getting into trouble for poking her nose into things that are not her business.

Pushka

Pushka is Mishki's brother. He loves adventure. He is always ready for a new challenge. Whether it's climbing a mountain, or diving into a cold, cold sea, he is up for it.

Daadu Dolma

Daadu Dolma is a wise old man who has lived on Earth longer than the mountains and the seas. No one knows quite how old he is, but he certainly has been around. He knows everything about everything.

Mishki and Pushka just can't sit still. They are going to one of the loveliest states in India.

'I've heard people say "God's own country" when they talk about this state,' says Pushka, jumping up and down. 'Why is that?'

'Probably because it has so much natural beauty that only God could have created it,' replies Daadu Dolma.

'And are there lots of beaches there? I love beaches!' says Mishki.

'Yes, there are. Beaches and the beautiful backwaters too,' answers Daadu.

'What are backwaters?' asks Pushka curiously.

'You will find out when we get there,' smiles Daadu. 'Are you packed and ready to go?'

'Yes, yes, yes!' shout Mishki and Pushka together. They are

OFF TO KERALA!!!

Land ahoy!

Oh, look, Daadu! The sea. I can't wait to dive in. What else is there in Kerala?

Patience, Mishki. There is a lot to see in Kerala apart from the sea. There are hills, plains and the unique backwaters. Let me tell you all about this wonderful state.

ON THE MAP

To see exactly where **Kerala** is on the map of India, go to

http://www.mapsofindia.com/maps/india/india-political-map.htm

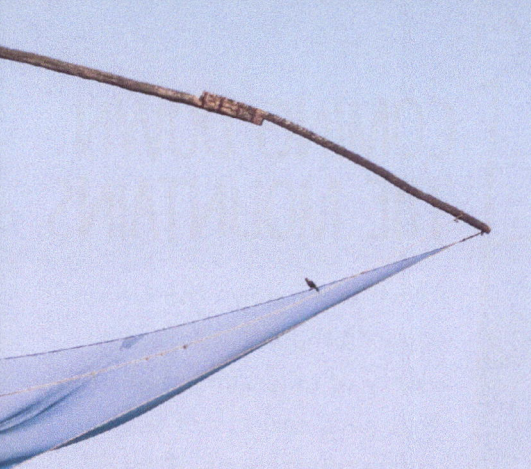

BEING NEIGHBOURLY

Kerala is a rather small state. It has many neighbours with whom it shares a lot of its history and traditions. Karnataka sits to its north, Tamil Nadu to its east and the Arabian Sea to its south and west.

A LONG, LONG COAST

You can imagine how long Kerala's coast is, with the sea to its south as well as west. This beautiful coast is called the Malabar Coast, which Kerala shares with Karnataka. Many people from European countries landed and mingled with the people here. That is why you will see that this state has a unique culture too!

Anai Peak

HILLY BILLY

The Western Ghats, that pass through many Indian states, run through the eastern part of Kerala too. The Anai Peak sits like a crown on the Ghats and is the highest peak in the entire range.

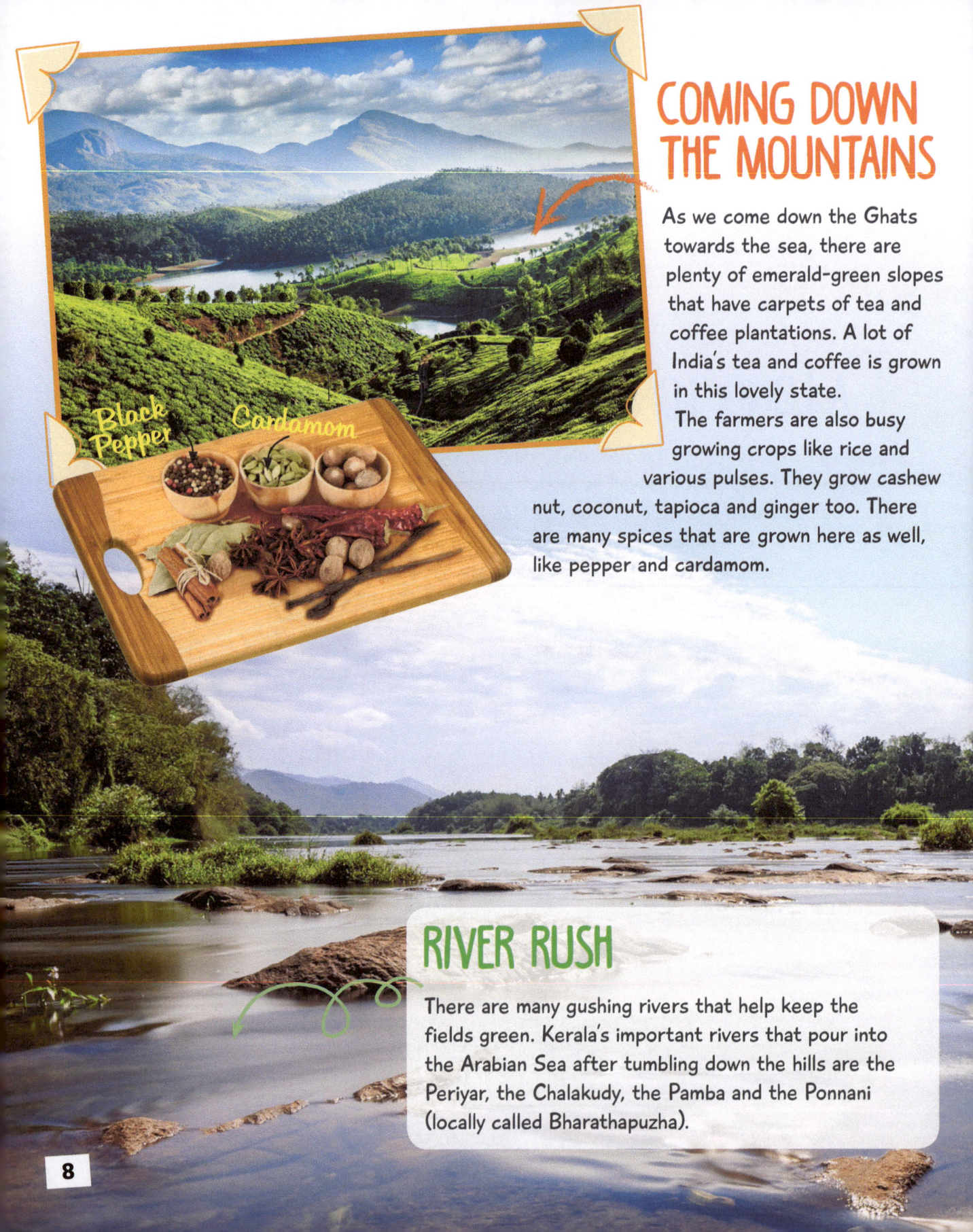

COMING DOWN THE MOUNTAINS

As we come down the Ghats towards the sea, there are plenty of emerald-green slopes that have carpets of tea and coffee plantations. A lot of India's tea and coffee is grown in this lovely state.

The farmers are also busy growing crops like rice and various pulses. They grow cashew nut, coconut, tapioca and ginger too. There are many spices that are grown here as well, like pepper and cardamom.

Black Pepper

Cardamom

RIVER RUSH

There are many gushing rivers that help keep the fields green. Kerala's important rivers that pour into the Arabian Sea after tumbling down the hills are the Periyar, the Chalakudy, the Pamba and the Ponnani (locally called Bharathapuzha).

COASTING ALONG

There are lots of fisherfolk in Kerala, owing to its long coastline. It is one of the largest fish-producing states. The main kinds of saltwater fish caught here are mackerels, sardines, tuna and prawns. That explains the yummy seafood that people in Kerala love.

Two monsoon seasons

A FRIENDLY CLIMATE

The climate of this state is as friendly as the people here. Not too hot, not too cold and sometimes wet. Kerala actually has two monsoon seasons. One arrives in June and the other in October. That's when the state becomes green and fresh. It's a lovely time to visit.

WHAT'S ODD?

In each row below, Mishki has found one word that doesn't belong. Can you circle it for her?

PRAWN	SARDINE	MACKEREL	WALRUS
CHALAKUDY	NILE	PAMBA	PONNANI
RICE	PULSES	BANYAN	CASHEW

FABULOUS FORESTS

The slopes of Kerala have some rich forests! The trees give us valuable wood, like ebony, teak and rosewood. They also have a lot of bamboo trees, which are an important raw material for many industries.

Teak forest

Nilgiri tahr

WILD AND WONDERFUL

The deep forests are home to some amazing wildlife, like gaurs, sambar deer, Nilgiri tahr, lion-tailed macaques, leopards, bonnet monkeys and a whole lot more.

Lion-tailed macaque

THE SILENT VALLEY

The Silent Valley is a beautiful evergreen forest in Kerala. It's home to some rare birds and animals. It almost got destroyed because a hydroelectric plant was going to be built in its place. But people protested so much that the forest and all the animals in it were saved. Now there is a lovely national park there.

State Flower
Golden shower

State Bird
Great Indian hornbill

State Tree
Coconut tree

State Animal
Elephant

Spot the Difference

Mishki has drawn what she thinks the Silent Valley looks like. So has Pushka. Can you find ten differences in the two pictures?

This doesn't look too silent, does it?

11

THE VENICE OF THE EAST

Ah! The famous Kerala backwaters! The rivers that pop in and out of the sea have created many lagoons, lakes and canals. Fringed by coconut trees smiling down on these canals, these are the backwaters of Kerala, in which you will see many houseboats floating along lazily, with people enjoying the calm environment.

The canals are so pretty that the place called Alappuzha, where many of these canals are, is called the Venice of the East.

A COMPLEX NETWORK

The entire backwater area is a complex network of large lakes that are connected to each other by canals. Some are natural and some are man made. There are many towns that you will see all along the backwater. It's not just tourists who come here to enjoy the peace. The canals are also used to transport cargo. And the water is used for irrigation too!

Transporting cargo

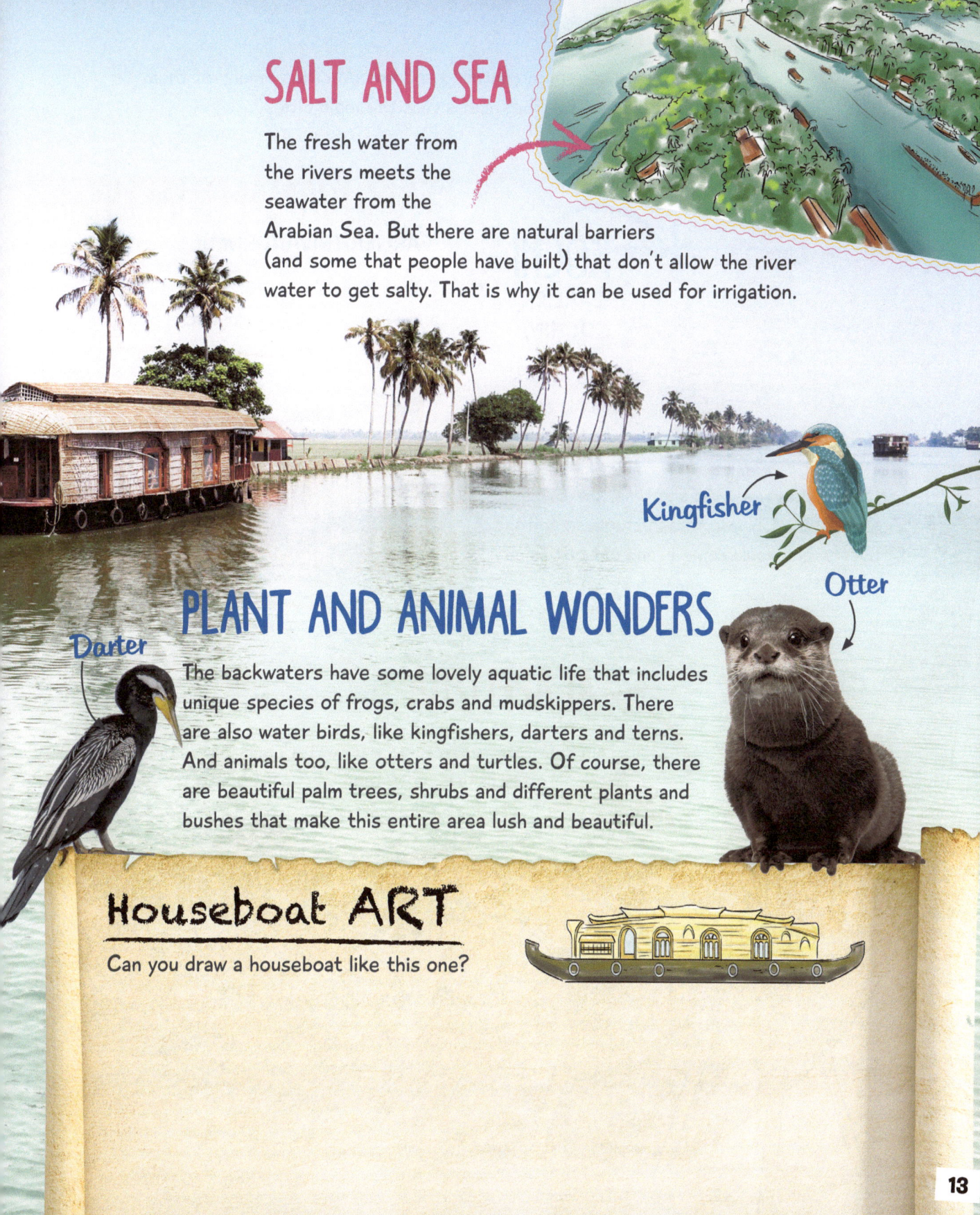

SALT AND SEA

The fresh water from the rivers meets the seawater from the Arabian Sea. But there are natural barriers (and some that people have built) that don't allow the river water to get salty. That is why it can be used for irrigation.

Kingfisher

Otter

PLANT AND ANIMAL WONDERS

Darter

The backwaters have some lovely aquatic life that includes unique species of frogs, crabs and mudskippers. There are also water birds, like kingfishers, darters and terns. And animals too, like otters and turtles. Of course, there are beautiful palm trees, shrubs and different plants and bushes that make this entire area lush and beautiful.

Houseboat ART

Can you draw a houseboat like this one?

Kerala has some charming and unique cities—many of them with lovely beaches. Let's visit the main cities.

CITY CITY BANG BANG

KOCHI
(EARLIER COCHIN)

This coastal city is said to have one of the nicest harbours in the world. At one time, the British, the Arabs, the Chinese, the Portuguese and the Dutch traders would come in and out of this city.

THIRUVANANTHAPURAM
(EARLIER TRIVANDRUM)

This is Kerala's capital. It has a long shoreline and some absolutely delightful beaches.

ALAPPUZHA (EARLIER ALLEPPEY)

In the heart of Kerala's backwaters sits this little jewel of a town. It is most famous for its boat races and houseboat holidays.

KOTTAYAM

This city has scenic beauty—with the Ghats on one side and the sea on the other. There are lots of paddy fields and rubber plantations here.

KOZHIKODE (EARLIER CALICUT)

Many years ago, this was one of the most important trading cities on the Malabar Coast. It has many lovely beaches, wildlife sanctuaries and friendly, warm people.

MUNNAR

Neelakurinji

Munnar is a picture-postcard town in the hills. The British used this as a summer resort when they ruled India. There is a blue flower called the *neelakurinji*, which blossoms every twelve years and turns all of the hills and valleys a brilliant shade of blue.

HIDDEN WORDS

How many words can you make from the word NEELAKURINJI? Mishki has made ten.
Suggestion: Write the letters in a mixed-up way and you will find words.

| N | E | E | L | A | K | U | R | I | N | J | I |

_____

_____ _____ _____

_____ _____ _____

Long, long ago

Daadu, you said that many people from different countries came here to trade. So did any of them stay back?

They did. And that's what makes Kerala very unusual. A lot of Kerala's history isn't written, but it's made of legends and stories. Come, let's go into the past to see Kerala's history.

FIRST-EVER MENTION

The first time in recorded history that Kerala was mentioned was on a rock inscription during the time of Emperor Ashoka. The word 'Keralaputra' can be seen inscribed on a rock as far back as the third-century BCE. That's a really, really long time ago.

Keralaputra was one of the five independent kingdoms that existed in India back during Emperor Ashoka's time.

SPICE IS NICE

Traders from the west loved the aromatic spices grown in Kerala. The Greeks, Romans and Dutch came in and out of Kerala, buying spices, especially pepper, to take back with them and sell. The Dutch even settled in this region for a while.

PART OF TAMILHAM

Once, Kerala was a part of Tamilham (which mainly had Tamil-speaking people). Today's Tamil Nadu, a part of Andhra Pradesh and Karnataka were also a part of this kingdom. The Pandya, Chola and Chera dynasties ruled this entire region during this time. But these dynasties fell apart to local forces.

SPICE ROUTE

These European boats are carrying spices back home with them. But they seem to have lost their way. Can you help them find it?

VISITORS FROM ACROSS THE SEA

RULED BY WARLORDS

The small chieftains and warlords fought each other for control. The Namboothiri clan, the Zamorin of Calicut, the Moopins of Perimpadappu and the chieftains of Kollam were all in for a major power struggle. This left the region weak and wide open for any strong power to take over. And that is exactly what the Portuguese did.

Christians, Muslims and Jews came from European and Arab countries to trade, and they landed on the shores of the Malabar Coast. Some of them stayed back and mixed with the local population. During this time, the region that is now Kerala was ruled by local chieftains and warlords who had overthrown the larger Chola and Chera kingdoms.

EUROPEAN RULE

For the next several hundred years, Kerala was ruled by first the Portuguese and then the Dutch. But the Dutch didn't last long. A local king called Marthanda Varma defeated them and tried his best to keep the state together under his rule. He did many good things for Kerala. But, by this time, the British has already advanced into Tamilham and had taken over much of India. They took over what were then called Cochin and Travancore (a part of present-day Kerala).

FIGHT FOR INDEPENDENCE

The whole country protested against the British. They wanted to be independent and not ruled by a foreign power. In 1947, India finally became independent. The new Indian government now began to rearrange the states to make the country more convenient to manage. Finally, the state of Kerala was born based on language. It was made up of people who spoke Malayalam.

WORD GRID

C	H	R	I	S	T	I	A	N	S	A
E	R	Z	T	Y	U	C	I	J	K	W
T	R	A	V	S	C	O	R	E	O	D
S	D	M	F	G	H	C	O	W	L	F
M	O	O	P	I	N	H	L	S	L	G
W	Q	R	L	K	J	I	A	R	A	B
E	R	I	T	Y	U	N	K	M	M	B
D	G	N	M	U	S	L	I	M	S	N

Can you find all these words hidden in the word grid? You can look from up to down and sideways too!

Christians, Muslims, Jews, Arab, Cochin, Moopins, Zamorin, Kollam

Daadu, I want to meet some people and talk to them. What language should I speak in?

Well, people in Kerala speak Malayalam, English and some Tamil too! But the main language is Malayalam, and it would be good to know some phrases in this language.

AN OLD, OLD LANGUAGE

Malayalam is a Dravidian language and the words are sometimes long and hard to pronounce, if you are not familiar with it. There is a lot of Sanskrit influence too! And here's something interesting—almost everyone in Kerala can speak or understand English.

Welcome = Swagatam

Hello = Namaskaram

How are you? = Enganuntu ninakku?

What is your name? = Ninte perentha?

Good morning = Suprabhatam

Goodbye = Ennal akatte

Sorry = Kshamikkanam

Thank you = Nanni

Please = Dayavai

Sit down = Irikku

Congratulations = Abhinandanangal

MATCH THE WORDS

Can you match the Malayalam words you have learnt to their English meanings?

Good morning   Please   Sit down   Welcome   Hello   Goodbye

Swagatam   Irikku   Namaskaram   Ennal akatte   Suprabhatam   Dayavai

A peep into their life

Oh, wow! Look at that amazing face-painting, Daadu. Can I paint my face like that? I would love to. What is that person doing?

That, Mishki, is a man who is preparing for a famous dance style called Kathakali, in which the dancers paint their faces. Kerala is full of very colourful festivals and dances. Come, let's see some of them. Then you can decide which one you want to do.

Text written on palm leaves

A CULTURED PEOPLE

The people of Kerala are very cultured—perhaps because education is very important to them. Did you know that Kerala has one of the highest literacy rates in India? That means more people in Kerala are educated than in other states. Literature, dance and music are also very important to the people here.

A LOVELY MIX

Mosque

Temple

Church

Though a majority of the people are Hindus, there are many Christians and Muslims here too, because of the Portuguese, Dutch and Arab influence. That is why the state has some beautiful churches, mosques and temples that we must see.

WELL-READ AND WRITTEN TOO!

With education being so important, it's only natural that the state has some rich literature. Malayalam is a beautiful language, and has amazing poetry. Thunchaththu Ezhuthachan and Kunchan Nambiar are famous classical poets. Centuries later, a writer called O. Chandu Menon wrote a book called *Indulekha*, which got him recognition.

Thunchaththu Ezhuthachan

AN ANCIENT MARTIAL ART

Kalaripayattu is an ancient martial art form that legends say Sage Parasurama innovated. It's a lot like kung fu, where the combatants draw from the poses and strength of snakes, crocodiles, elephants, wild boars and so on. The Chola, Chera and Pandya dynasties based their fighting techniques on it. It was taught to students by Kalaripayattu masters in totally secrecy. Now, people perform it as an art form.

DANCE DANCE DANCE

Kerala has some of India's most colourful and famous dances. Let's see some of them.

MOHINIYATTAM

This is a classical and very beautiful form of dance performed by women. There are bits of this dance that remind you of other dances, like Bharatanatyam. Facial expressions are important in this style, and dancers use their eyes very expressively.

KATHAKALI

This fascinating dance is usually performed by men. They paint their faces dramatically and wear billowing skirts. The dancers play the role of characters from epics—the Ramayana and the Mahabharata. And these stories are depicted entirely through dance.

OTTAMTHULLAL

This is a theatrical dance performance that is very old. Originally, a single performer, wearing heavy make-up and a colourful costume, would tell stories. Now, groups perform this and it is very popular.

THIRUVATHIRAKALI

This fun dance is performed in groups during the festival of Onam. Women dance in a circle to the tune of traditional songs.

KOLKALI

The farming community mainly performs this dance. The dancers move in a circle, banging long wooden sticks on the ground to a rhythmic beat.

Wooden sticks

TWIN MASKS

Mishki has painted some Kathakali masks. Can you find two masks that are exactly the same?

A

B

C

D

FANTASTIC FESTIVALS

Kerala has some really unique festivals that involve prayer, sport, celebration and loads of fun. Let's look at some amazing festivals of this state.

Onam sadya

OH! IT'S ONAM!

This harvest festival is probably Kerala's most important one. Legend says that the festival celebrates the arrival of King Mahabali, a much loved king who had been away from his subjects for some time. People decorate the front of their house with a pattern of flowers called *pookalam*. A yummy meal called *Onam sadya* (consisting of almost fifteen dishes) is cooked. People also enjoy the famous boat races in nearby towns. It's a fun celebration, all right.

King Mahabali

V FOR VISHU

People believe that the first person who visits them on the morning of Vishu, Kerala's New Year, will bring them good fortune. They prepare a *kani*, which is the first thing they see when they wake up. The *kani* is made of gold ornaments and mirrors, with flowers and fruits. Two oil lamps stand next to it. People believe this is very auspicious.

DAZZLING BOAT RACES

The boat race festivals of Kerala are so famous that people come to see them from all over the world. There are many races held in the different lakes and rivers, but one of the oldest is the Aranmula Uthrattathi boat race. Hundreds of oarsmen take the oars of boats that are shaped like a snake. They row furiously, singing songs to keep their rhythm going. There are water processions, colourful floats and decorated boats that make this festival truly magnificent.

People say that in the olden days, kings settled disputes with a boat race to decide the winner.

PASSIONATE ABOUT POORAM

Pooram is celebrated in temples across Kerala. The Thrissur Pooram is probably one of Kerala's biggest. The highlight is the procession of gaily decorated elephants, followed by a traditional ceremony called kudamattam. Devotees and visitors unfurl thousands of colourful umbrellas. It's an awesome sight.

BOAT RACE FUN

Spot ten differences between these two pictures of a boat race.

Bricks and Stones

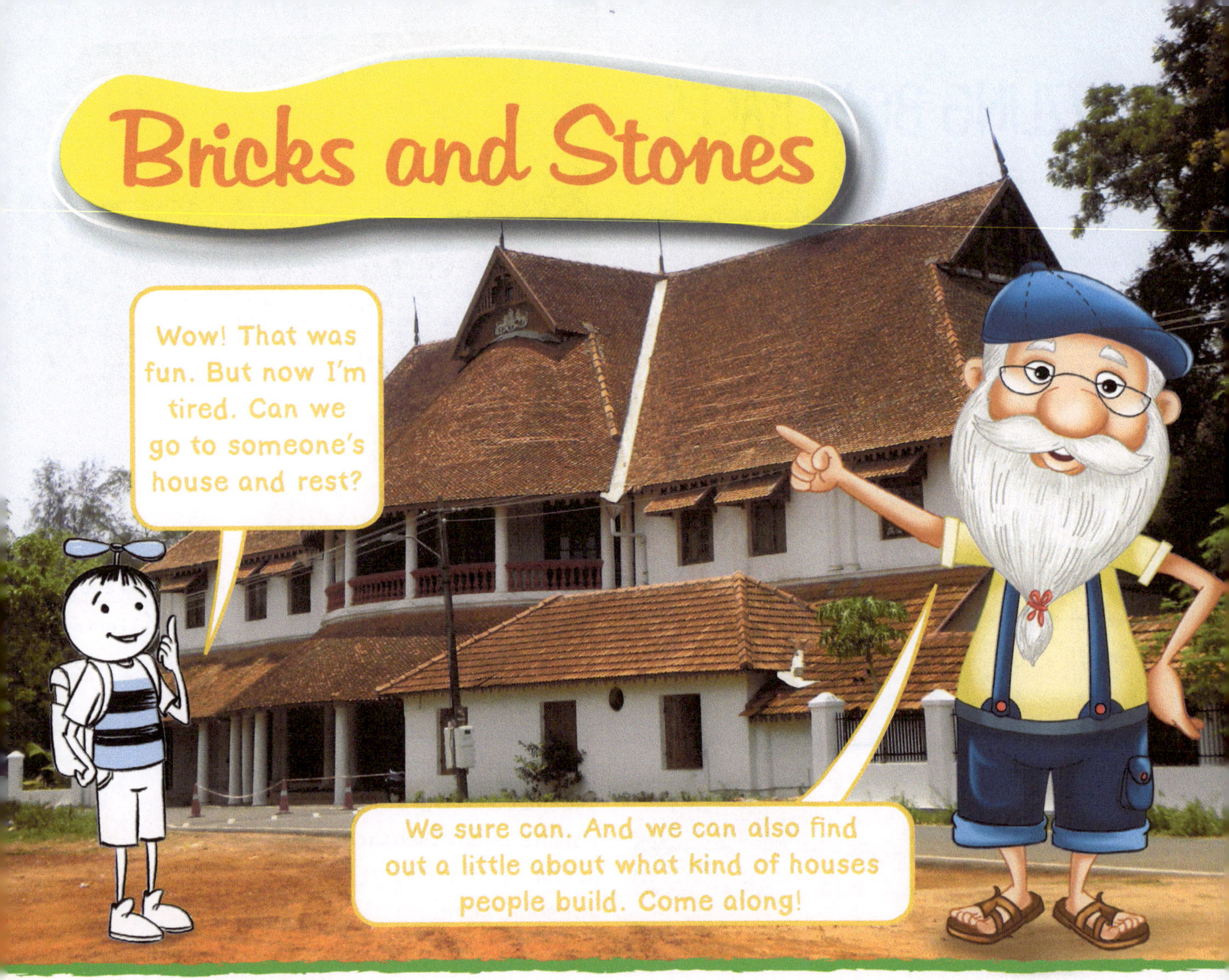

Wow! That was fun. But now I'm tired. Can we go to someone's house and rest?

We sure can. And we can also find out a little about what kind of houses people build. Come along!

ECO-FRIENDLY HOMES

In ancient times, houses were built to suit the humid climate of Kerala. The materials that people could find easily were timber, clay, stones (like granite) and palm leaves. The houses had low roofs that sheltered them from rain and sun. A veranda around the house is where the family would collect.

Kerala's local architecture is very different from the rest of India.

Deep veranda

WONDERFUL VEEDUS

The houses in Kerala are called *veedus*, where large joint families lived happily together. The joint family system was called *tharavad*. The houses were enormous and had plenty of space for uncles, aunts, cousins and grandparents. Must have been fun!

FLOORED!!!

Just think of how imaginative the people of Kerala were. In most houses, the floor was made of mud that was beaten and mixed with cow dung. This kept the floor cool and clean. But in the more expensive houses, people actually made a mixture of sand, lime, coconut water, egg whites and vegetable juices.

Floor=Sand+Lime+Egg whites  +Coconut water

JUMBLED WORDS

Can you unscramble the names of the materials that people in Kerala use to build their homes?

BITREM - _____ (a kind of wood)

YALC - _____ (a material like mud)

NIGARTE - _____ (a kind of stone)

ALMP - _____ (a tree with leaves that are useful)

Large verandas

THE HOUSES OF THE PAST

At one time, in some parts of Kerala, big traditional houses called *nalukettu* were common. They were very scientifically built. Teak wood and wood from jackfruit trees were the main materials. The roof would be made of dried palm leaves. The houses would have space for a granary to store grains, with ponds and wells for water and large verandas to chill out in.

Ponds

Granary

COURTYARD TALES

Usually at the centre of the house, the courtyard had many functions. It was a place for prayer, and often had a holy tulsi plant growing in it. It was also a place for community activities and an extension of the kitchen, where family members carried out chores like pickling and cleaning grain. The courtyard usually had four halls surrounding it, for storing grains, cooking, dining and sleeping. How cosy it all sounds!

BIG HOUSES

Many traditional houses had more than one storey. The second storey was more like an attic and had gabled windows. This allowed a breeze to flow through the attic. See how imaginative people were?

A typical attic in a traditional house

BLOCKY PUZZLE

Help Mishki fill in all the squares. In the orange squares you will find a word which means a type of window.

(The place where people stored grains)

(Another word for a balcony)

(Windows were designed to let this in)

(The holy plant in the centre of the house)

(Wells were needed for people to get this)

Standing strong

Daadu, I am loving Kerala. I think it's so different from many other states. What kind of monuments does it have?

Kerala has an interesting mixture of monuments. Because so many foreign powers made this their home, the monuments are a lovely mix of Hindu, Jewish, Christian and Islamic monuments. Let's visit some.

FANTASTIC FORTS

THE BEKAL FORT

This lovely fort is one of Kerala's largest. It is shaped like a giant keyhole. It has massive observation towers from where soldiers could spot enemies approaching from miles away. It even has a Hanuman temple and a mosque inside it.

ANJUTHENGU FORT

The word *anjuthengu* means five coconut trees. You guessed right. There are many coconut groves close to this fort, which is what must have given it its name. The British used it as a trading hub. This area also has the graves of British soldiers who died here.

THALASSERY FORT

This fort was built by the British to keep an eye on the Malabar Coast. It has many carved doors, secret tunnels and underground rooms. It even has a pier that leads you right out to the sea. It must have been exciting to live in those times!

Secret tunnels

PALAKKAD FORT

This fort was built by Hyder Ali, father of the famous warrior Tipu Sultan, when he ruled this part of Kerala for a short time. It was here that Tipu bravely fought a war against the British before losing to them.

TEMPLE BELLS

JEWISH SYNAGOGUE

Many Jewish people settled in Kerala, from where they carried on a brisk trade. They built lots of houses of worship. The most famous is the Paradesi Synagogue in Kochi. One of the oldest in India, it has Chinese tiles, delicate Belgian glass and old copper plates decorating the walls.

A Jewish temple is called a synagogue.

Belgian glass

Chinese tiles

THIRUNELLI TEMPLE

This ancient temple is dedicated to Lord Vishnu. It has a lovely location, and is surrounded by mountains and forests. It even has a river called Papanasini flowing past it. People believe that this river washes away their sins. This temple attracts a large number of visitors.

Papanasini actually means one who will wash away sins.

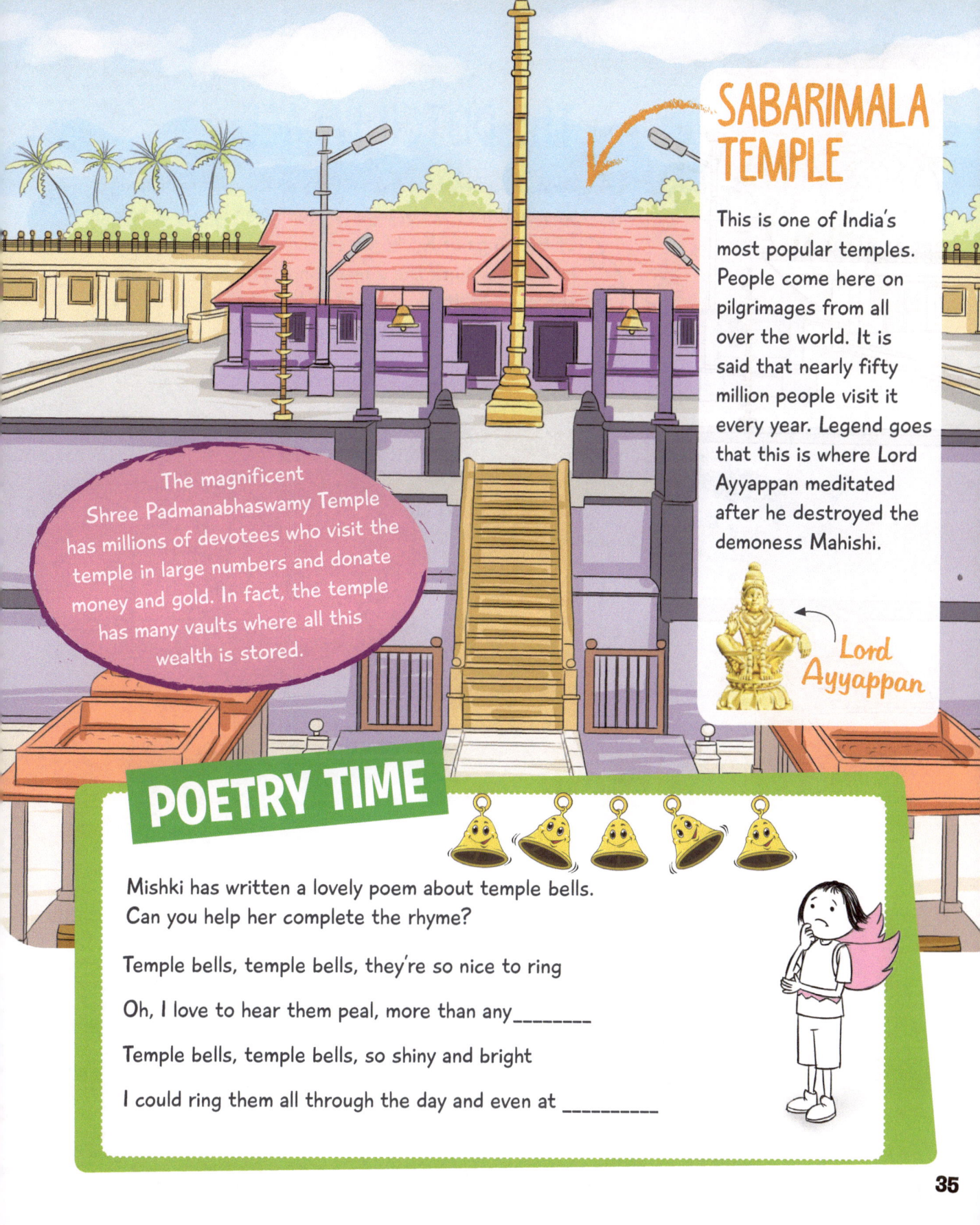

SABARIMALA TEMPLE

This is one of India's most popular temples. People come here on pilgrimages from all over the world. It is said that nearly fifty million people visit it every year. Legend goes that this is where Lord Ayyappan meditated after he destroyed the demoness Mahishi.

Lord Ayyappan

The magnificent Shree Padmanabhaswamy Temple has millions of devotees who visit the temple in large numbers and donate money and gold. In fact, the temple has many vaults where all this wealth is stored.

POETRY TIME

Mishki has written a lovely poem about temple bells. Can you help her complete the rhyme?

Temple bells, temple bells, they're so nice to ring

Oh, I love to hear them peal, more than any _____

Temple bells, temple bells, so shiny and bright

I could ring them all through the day and even at _____

PALACE PERFECTION

THE DUTCH PALACE

Also called Mattancherry Palace, this lovely building was built by the Portuguese and given as a gift to one of the kings of Kochi. Later, the Dutch redesigned it. It looks more like a mansion than a palace from the outside. It has a temple inside it and lots of royal objects on display—like weapons, swings and furniture.

BOLGATTY PALACE

Yet another Dutch palace, this is one of the oldest outside of Holland. It is on an island in the middle of the Arabian Sea. Now it has been converted into a hotel with lavish rooms. People from around the world come to stay here and get a taste of how royalty lived.

KRISHNAPURAM PALACE

This palace was built by a man called Anizham Thirunal Marthanda Varma. It is full of all kinds of objects from hundreds of years ago. There is even a museum here, which has sculptures, weapons, paintings, stone inscriptions, coins and lots more.

Weapons in the museum

THE HILL PALACE

The royal family of Kochi still owns this delightful palace. This huge palace has its own deer park and horses you can ride, as well as a museum where you can see rare paintings, stone sculptures, ancient weapons, coins and a lot more. What an interesting place this must be!

Ride a horse

I am going to see this for sure. I love riding horses!

GIANT CROSSWORD

Mishki and Pushka have learnt so much. They want to see how much they remember. Can you help them solve this giant crossword?

ACROSS

2. A Jewish temple
3. The palace built by Anizham Thirunal Marthanda Varma
5. A monument that kings built to defend their kingdom
7. The long Kerala coast which the British wanted to keep an eye on
8. The Papanasini river washes these away
10. The delicate glass from a European country
12. Underground corridors
13. The person who prays at a synagogue
14. One of Kerala's largest forts
15. The demoness that Lord Ayyappan killed
16. The Thirunelli temple is dedicated to this god
17. The shape of Bekal Fort

DOWN

1. The tree commonly found in Kerala.
2. Nearly fifty million people visit this temple every year
3. Mattancherry Palace was given as a gift to a king of _____
4. The royal family of Cochin still own this palace
6. Hyder Ali's son who was a brave warrior
9. The place in a palace which has sculptures, weapons, paintings, stone inscriptions, coins and lots more
10. The people who ruled India till Independence
11. The people who built a palace named after themselves

GIANT MAZE

Mishki and Pushka can't find Daadu Dolma. Help them find their way to him.

Working hard

You told us that almost all the people in Kerala are educated and can read and write too! Do they work just as hard, Daadu?

You got that right. People are hardworking in Kerala and they do a lot of things. Let's meet some people and see what they do for a living in this lovely state.

FARMER, FARMER, WHAT DO YOU GROW?

We've already seen that Kerala is so green and has lots of farms. So, naturally, many people here are farmers. They grow lots of different crops—right from rice, pulses and tapioca to cashews, cardamom and pepper. And many others things too!

The spices grown in Kerala are world famous. Even hundreds of years ago, the Portuguese and the Dutch bought spices from here to take back to Europe. The Romans too loved Kerala's spices.

Coffee beans

BREWS AND BREWS

The coffee and tea plantations in Kerala not only give people employment, but are so beautiful that tourists come here to visit the gardens. There are people who work in these gardens to pick the tea; there are also thousands of people who work in the factories where tea and coffee is processed.

There is a tea museum in Munnar, where you can see how tea is made and taste many different kinds of tea.

LET'S GO FISHING

Kerala has such a long coastline that fish is one of the staple foods. So there are lots of fishermen and fish production in this state. In fact, Kerala is one of India's largest fish-producing states. This has also given rise to a large food-processing industry.

SOMETHING'S FISHY

Pushka wants to go fishing. But wait! Is this just one fish or are there many hidden in it? Count the fish and help Pushka out.

Wind farms

LIGHTING UP LIVES

There are more than twenty massive hydroelectric stations in Kerala, where electricity is produced. There are also many wind farms. Lots of people work in these places to generate electricity and light up lives.

Aranmula mirror

WOODY WOOD WOOD

The thick forests of Kerala give us a lot of valuable wood, like ebony, rosewood, teak and bamboo. Forestry is, therefore, an important occupation. Cutting trees so that the forests aren't harmed and converting them into usable things is what forestry entails.

HANDY HANDICRAFT

For generations, people in Kerala have been hand-making objects of great beauty. They make magnificent metal bells and lamps; many types of coir and cane items; sandalwood objects for the house; wooden toys; and beautifully woven silk saris as well.

CENTRES OF HEALING

Ayurveda is an ancient science of healing the body with natural materials. Kerala is India's leading state in the art of Ayurveda. There are many Ayurvedic centres where people work as doctors and masseurs. These massages make people feel as good as new!

TOURIST PARADISE

Kerala has millions of tourists that come here to see the monuments, enjoy the backwaters, go on pilgrimages or take care of their health. So the tourism industry—airlines, hotels and restaurants—keep a lot of people very busy indeed.

I want to stay in a houseboat hotel.

Yum yum yum

Daadu, there's a rumble in my tummy. I'm sooooo hungry. What kind of food are we going to eat?

I'm glad you're hungry. Cuisine from Kerala is famous around the world. But, mind you, it can be spicy! Let's get going on our food journey.

COCONUTTY

You will love the flavours of Kerala's food. There's coconut in most dishes, and it is made even more tasty with chilli, tamarind, mustard and all sorts of fragrant spices that are grown in the state.

MEEN PEERA

Meen means fish in Malayalam. *Meen peera* is a yummy dish of fish immersed in a tasty mixture of coconut and fragrant spices. It's a dry dish that people love to have with *kanji* (a kind of rice soup).

Kanji

AVIAL

This dish is as healthy as it is tasty. It has got a lot of vegetables that are cooked in a delectable mix of coconut and spices. People eat it with rice and sambar.

KARIKKU PAYASAM

Karikku means tender coconut. Karikku payasam is a delicious pudding made with coconut water and soft coconut flesh—all mixed with milk, sugar and nuts. Yummmmm!

KOOTUCURRY

Whenever there's a feast, there is bound to be *kootucurry* on the menu. *Kootu* means mixing up. This dish is made by mixing up lots of pulses with different vegetables, banana, yam and winter melon. It tastes super with rice.

Vegetables + Pulses = Kootu

45

APPAM AND STEW

This hugely popular dish has a touch of Europe in it. Appams are pancakes with a plump centre. And the stew is a delicious coconut-based gravy with either meat or vegetables. This is a popular breakfast dish, but now people serve it at weddings and other celebrations too!

Stew

Appam

Pancake

Sweet + Sour

PULLISERY

This is a yummy side dish that people make with different vegetables or fruit. Cucumber, pineapple, or raw or sweet mango taste the best in this sweet-and-sour curd-based dish.

PUTTU

This is Kerala's favourite breakfast dish. These little rice cylinders are made of rice flour and coconut. You need a special vessel called a *puttu kutti* in order to steam the *puttu*. People eat this with a special curry called *kadala curry*.

Puttu kutti

CHIP CHOP

Kerala's favourite munchies are chips. Because there are so many banana and jackfruit trees, people dry the fruits and make delicious chips using them. They are called *chakka varuthadu*. Banana chips are called *nendra kaya varuthadu* and are made from raw, green bananas. People from all over India love crunching on these at any time of the day.

Nendra kaya varuthadu

CRUNCH!
CRUNCH!

Chakka varuthadu

FOOD GRID

Pushka is still hungry. Help him find the names of the dishes of Kerala.

P	U	L	L	I	S	E	R	Y	A
Q	W	E	R	C	H	I	P	S	C
A	P	P	A	M	E	S	T	E	W
A	S	D	F	P	U	T	T	U	V
A	V	I	A	L	U	H	M	N	B
K	O	O	T	U	C	U	R	R	Y

What to wear?

Daadu, I want to dress up in traditional clothes from Kerala. What should I wear?

You'll look great in the clothing from this state. People from Kerala wear simple but elegant clothes. Come, let me show you.

ALL WHITE

You could say that when it comes to clothes, white is Kerala's favourite colour. The traditional clothing for both men and women is mainly white. But it's not dull at all. It usually has a touch of gold, making it look very classy.

Kara

LOVELY DRAPE

Women traditionally wore something called a *mundum neriyathum*. This basically consists of two long pieces of cloth—one draped around the hips, and the other like a sari. The glowing golden border is called a *kara*.

MUNDU MAGIC

The traditional clothing for men is just as elegant and simple. They too wear a *mundu* (the long cloth) draped around their waist. They wear this with a shirt or a kurta.

Mundu

Idols of gods

GOLD IS NEVER OLD

The golden ornaments from Kerala are famous, and women from all over India love them—especially the neckpieces. Each type of necklace has a different name. This temple-inspired jewellery is also put on the idols of gods.

MODERN TIMES

Just like the rest of India, most men and women now wear this traditional attire during weddings and other festivals. At other times, they wear modern clothes like jeans, T-shirts and salwaar kameez.

WHAT'S ODD?

In each row, there is one odd word that doesn't belong. Can you circle it?

JEANS	T-SHIRT	SHORTS	MUNDU
WHITE	GOLD	SKY	SILVER
SHIRT	JACKET	MUNDUM	BLOUSE

Autograph, please?

I love to meet new people. Who are you going to introduce us to?

There are many learned and talented people from Kerala. Some of them don't live there anymore, but they are very much considered Keralites. I'm going to get you to meet just a few of them.

ADI SHANKARA

He was a great philosopher who is believed to have established the base of Hinduism as we know it. He travelled across India, spreading his philosophy through debates with other thinkers. He has many thousands of disciples who follow his teachings even today.

JYESTHADEVA

He was a great astronomer and mathematician who lived hundreds of years ago. He wrote many books on both these subjects that have become the basis for some theorems as well.

VERGHESE KURIEN

This visionary was called the Father of the White Revolution in India. He set up an entire milk cooperative in Gujarat to help the farmers. It gave rise to the famous brand Amul—which today not only has milk but all kinds of cheese, yoghurt and other dairy products as well.

RAJA RAVI VARMA

He was an amazing painter who came from a family of artists and poets. His style of painting people was unique, and many artists have been inspired by him. His paintings are displayed in many homes and galleries across the world.

K.J. YESUDAS

This incredible singer has sung in virtually all the Indian languages and in foreign languages like Russian, Arabic, English and Latin too! He sings classical songs, devotional songs and movie songs.

P.T. USHA

She is the superfast athlete who was nicknamed Payyoli Express because she ran so fast. She took part in the Olympics and has won many medals in various championships.

ADOOR GOPALAKRISHNAN

He is a famous director who has made movies that have earned him many awards and lots of international recognition.

ABU ABRAHAM

He was a famous cartoonist, journalist and writer, whose work was published in many Indian and international publications.

MATCH

THEM RIGHT

Match the famous person to what he or she is famous for.

Abu Abraham	Famous painter
P.T. Usha	The White Revolution
Raja Ravi Varma	Singer
Jyesthadeva	Cartoonist
K.J. Yesudas	Mathematician
Verghese Kurien	Athlete

53

Once upon a time . . .

I simply love Kerala. But I'm tired now. Daadu, will you tell us a nice story from this state?

Yes, I will. Come and sit by my side. I will tell you a story about why Kerala has so many coconut trees.

THE GIRL AND THE COCONUT TREE

There was a young girl called Kanaka. She lived with her father and mother in a little house by the sea. Kanaka loved nothing more than sitting on the sand or going into the water to paddle.

She would spend hours and hours looking at the waves. Sometimes she would collect shells to take home with her and decorate her house.

The creatures in the sea loved her very much, for she was always kind and gentle. She would feed the turtles when they came out to sun themselves on the rocks.
She would be careful to never hurt the little crabs that scurried around her feet while she walked on the sand.

Kanaka was very happy living by the sea, even though she and her family had very little. You see, they were rather poor. Her father was a fisherman who hated catching fish. But he had no choice. He had to earn something to feed his family.

One day, Kanaka was sitting on a rock, gazing at the horizon. She was thinking hard about what she could do to help her father earn some money. Suddenly, she saw something glistening on the sand.

I wonder what that is, she thought. She went to take a closer look. To her surprise, it was an eel—a creature she had never seen before. It was long and slippery, a cross between a snake and a fish.

'Oh, you poor little thing!' cried Kanaka. 'You're stuck on the sand. I will take you back into the water.' She picked up the creature. It wriggled and slithered in her hand, for it was a slippery thing. She waded into the water and when it was deep enough, she gently slipped it back into the sea.

The creature swam away. Kanaka went home and forgot all about it.

The next morning, Kanaka was helping her mother fill water. There was a knock on the door.

'See who it is, Kanaka,' her mother called out. Kanaka opened her door.

There was no one there. She looked down. To her amazement, the slippery creature was on the ground.

'Oh, what are you doing here?' Kanaka exclaimed. She bent down and was about to pick it up, when something strange happened. The creature disappeared and in his place stood a handsome man.

Kanaka gaped in amazement. 'Do not be afraid,' the man said, smiling. 'I am the god of eels. I saw how you helped me yesterday on the beach. And I want to give you a gift. When I leave, you will find some seeds below your mat. Bury those seeds and you will soon see my gift.' Saying that, he disappeared.

Kanaka looked under the mat. Sure enough, there were some strange seeds there. As she had been told, she buried them in the back garden. Some months later, to her surprise, a sapling had popped out of the ground. Kanaka watered the sapling and cared for it. Soon, it grew into a tall coconut tree.

The tree swayed in the wind. It bore coconuts full of fresh sweet water and rich white flesh. She made mats from its leaves. And Kanaka's father sold the coconuts in the market. Soon, they were not poor any more.

This really was a wonderful gift, thought Kanaka, thinking affectionately of the eel.

This is why people in Kerala believe that the coconut tree, with every part being useful, is a gift from the god of eels. They say that when you remove the fibre from the coconut, you can see the face of the eel, its eyes and its nose too!

TRAVEL DIARY

Have you enjoyed this trip to Kerala with your friends Mishki and Pushka—and, of course, with Daadu Dolma?

Now you can make your own Kerala diary. And if you ever visit Kerala, make sure you take pictures and put them in the photo box.

The first place I would visit in Kerala:

_____

If I ever meet P.T. Usha, this is what I would like to ask her:

_____

The one dish I am definitely going to eat:

_____

The monument I think is the most interesting:

_____

The one famous person from Kerala I would love to meet:

_____

If I lived in Kerala, this is the work I would like to do:

_____

The festival from Kerala that I think is the most fun:

_____

The five words that I think describe Kerala the best are:

_____

_____

_____

_____

_____

My Kerala memories:

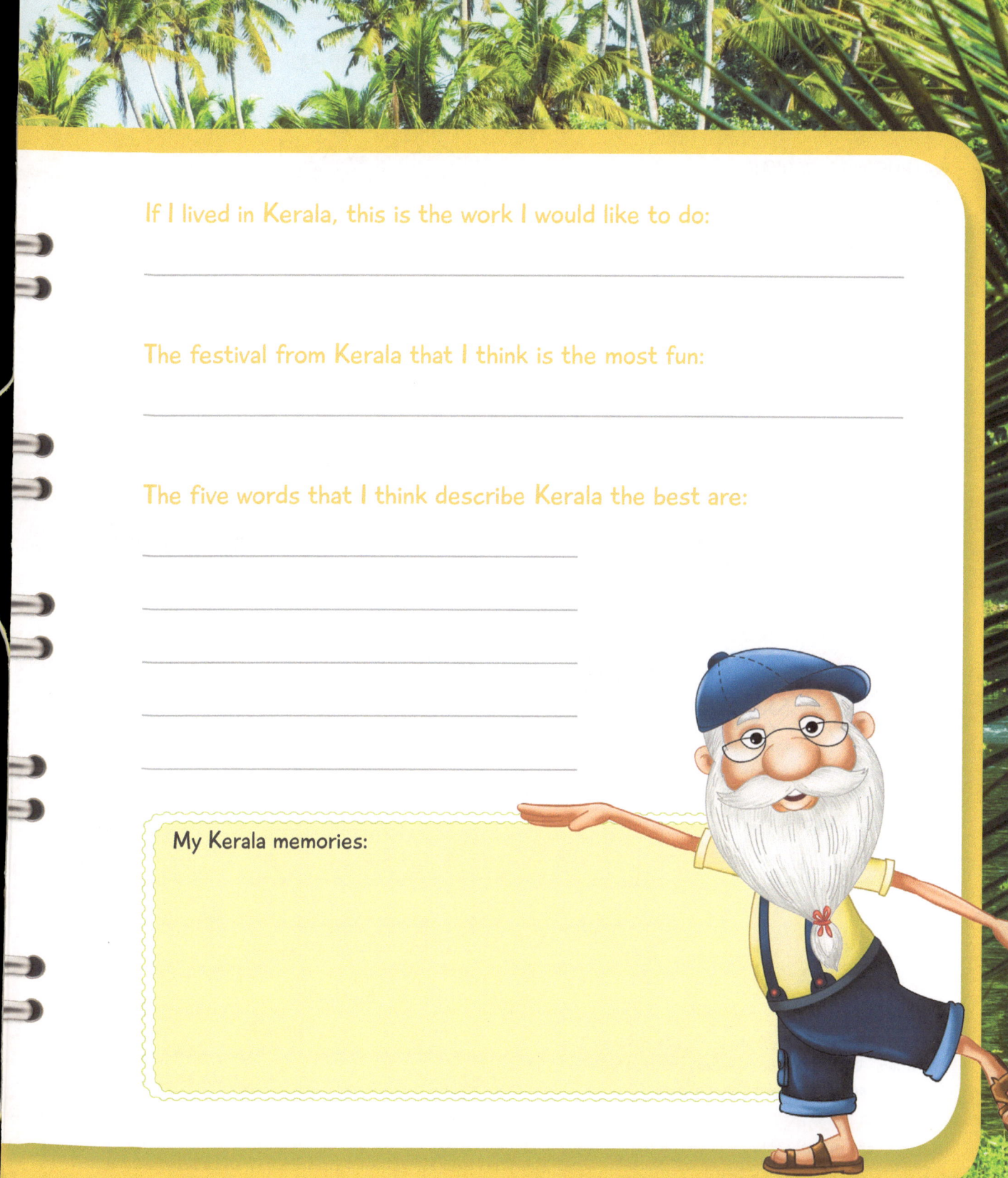

ANSWERS

page 9 WHAT'S ODD
WALRUS, NILE, BANYAN

page 11 SPOT THE DIFFERENCE

page 15 HIDDEN WORDS
Here are some of the words you can form: are, ear, eel, elk, ink, inn, jar, lie, nun, raj, ran, run, urn, earn, jail, jerk, juke, junk, kale, keel, keen, knee, lark, leak, like, line, lure, nail, near, nine, rail, rain, rake, rank, real, reek, reel, rile, rink, ruin, rule

page 17 SPICE ROUTE

page 19 WORD GRID

C	H	R	I	S	T	I	A	N	S	A
E	R	Z	T	Y	U	C	I	J	K	W
T	R	A	V	S	C	O	R	E	O	D
S	D	M	F	G	H	C	O	W	L	F
M	O	O	P	I	N	H	L	S	L	G
W	Q	R	L	K	J	I	A	R	A	B
E	R	I	T	Y	U	N	K	M	M	B
D	G	N	M	U	S	L	I	M	S	N

page 21 MATCH THE WORDS
Good morning—Suprabhatam; Please—Dayavai; Sit down—Irikku; Welcome—Swagatam; Hello—Namaskaram; Goodbye—Ennal akatte

page 25 TWIN MASKS
B and D are exactly alike.

page 27 BOAT RACE FUN

page 29 JUMBLED WORDS
TIMBER, CLAY, GRANITE, PALM

page 31 BLOCKY PUZZLE
GRANARY, VERANDA, BREEZE, TULSI, WATER, GABLE

page 35 POETRY TIME
thing, night

page 38 GIANT CROSSWORD

page 39 GIANT MAZE

page 41 SOMETHING's FISHY
Thirty-nine

page 47 FOOD GRID

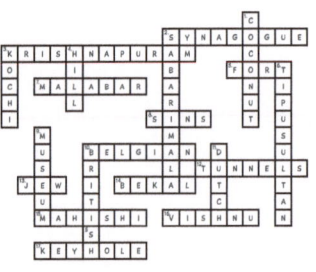

P	U	L	L	I	S	E	R	Y	A
Q	W	E	R	C	H	I	P	S	C
A	P	P	A	M	E	S	T	E	W
A	S	D	F	P	U	T	T	U	V
A	V	I	A	L	U	H	M	N	B
K	O	O	T	U	C	U	R	R	Y

page 49 ODD ONE OUT
MUNDU, SKY, MUNDUM

page 53 MATCH THEM RIGHT
Abu Abraham—Cartoonist; PT Usha—Athlete; Raja Ravi Varma—Famous Painter; Jyesthadeva—Mathematician; Yesudas—Singer; Verghese Kurien—The White Revolution